P9-EKS-722
CANBY PUBLIC LIBRARY
292 N HOLLY
CANBY OR 97013

Translator - Alexander O. Smith
Script Editor - Rich Amtower
Retouch and Lettering - Patrick Tran
Cover Design - Raymond Makowski
Graphic Designer - John Lo

Editor - Jake Forbes
Digital Imaging Manager - Chris Buford
Pre-Press Manager - Antonio DePietro
Production Managers - Jennifer Miller, Mutsumi Miyazaki
Art Director - Matt Alford
Managing Editor - Jill Freshney
VP of Production - Ron Klamert
President & C.O.O. - John Parker
Publisher & C.E.O. - Stuart Levy

E-mail: info@TOKYOPOP.com
Come visit us online at www.TOKYOPOP.com

A  Manga

TOKYOPOP Inc.
5900 Wilshire Blvd. Suite 2000
Los Angeles, CA 90036

Samurai Deeper Kyo Vol. 7

©2000 Akimine Kamijyo. All rights reserved.
First published in Japan in 2000 by Kodansha LTD., Tokyo.
English language translation rights arranged by Kodansha LTD.

English text copyright ©2004 TOKYOPOP Inc.

All rights reserved. No portion of this book may be reproduced or transmitted in any form or by any means without written permission from the copyright holders. This manga is a work of fiction. Any resemblance to actual events or locales or persons, living or dead, is entirely coincidental.

ISBN: 1-59182-543-1

First TOKYOPOP printing: June 2004

10 9 8 7 6 5 4 3 2 1
Printed in the USA

Vol. 7

by Akimine Kamijyo

Los Angeles • Tokyo • London • Hamburg

DRAMATIS PERSONAE

...According to Tora.

The deadliest samurai, said to have killed **1,000** men. With a past like his, there are plenty of people who want him dead.

The mysterious man after Kyo-han's life! Who is he?!

(Former Friends Rivalry Curiosity)

(Master)

ed)

The
ame
uy)

Former friend of Kyo-han. One of the "Four Emperors."

The Twelve

Twelve God Shoguns--samurai who protect THE MASTER.

? ? ?

That bastard who killed Yuya-han's brother.

Super muscled, but talks like a girl.

She's cute, yeah, but she's also freakin' deadly!

A real looker. Immortal, too.

An archer. Calls himself "Maro."

A real meanie. The "ends justifies the means" type.

He was definitely the smartest of the Twelve.

I'LL TEACH YA GOOD!
Benitora Sensei
SAMURAI DEEPE
KYO
BENITORA (Tokugawa Hidetada)
"Benitora the Shadow Man" Give me a spear and I'll lick anybody!
(Curiosity)
MIBU KYOSHIR
(Love! ♡ I hope...)
Don't let that baby face fool you--he's strong enough to beat Kyo-han. Still, he looks like a wimp.
SANADA YUKI-MURA
(Friends?)
Sweet Sanada, after my dad's head.
(Rivals)
(Punching Bag)
Fill-in fo Sakuya
(Master)
SANADA'S TEN
Ten warriors serving the Sanada House.
SASUKE (Sarutobi Sasuke)
Little ninja, raised in Aokigahara.
(Love! ♡)
SHIINA YUYA
(Amorous? Bounty Hunter)
My true (puppy) love. She hunts bounties and seeks to avenge her brother. I love it when she plays tough!

Kyo and company have made their way to the forest of **Aokigahara** at the base of Mt. Fuji, the place where Kyo's body is said to be frozen in ice.

Also in the forest are the **Twelve God Shoguns**, an elite team of samurai called into action by their leader, **The Master**.

Soon upon entering, Kyo and Yuya become separated from Benitora and Okuni.

Elsewhere in the forest, Kyo finds what appears to be the **cave** where his body is buried.

...but it's actually a trap created by **Kubira** the Puppeteer, smartest of the Twelve.

Kubira drags the battle on past Kyo's ten minute limit, but then something completely unexpected happens...

Kyo and Benitora defeat their enemies, but the other members of the Twelve are still at large.

Meanwhile, from his base in Kudoyama, **Sanada Yukimura** sets off for Aokigahara with an agend of his own...

...but his arrival is preceded by a meeting with **Sasuke** of the **Sanada Ten** who makes Kyo an offer...

SAMURAI DEEPER KYO

TABLE OF CONTENTS

CHAPTER 51 ✠ THE DEMON-BLADE MURAMASA 9
CHAPTER 52 ✠ VISITOR ON A DARK NIGHT 30
CHAPTER 53 ✠ THE BIGGEST DUMMY IN THE WORLD 51
CHAPTER 54 ✠ DEMON EYES DEFEAT 71
CHAPTER 55 ✠ THE DEMONS HEARTBEAT 91
CHAPTER 56 ✠ DEMON EYES OPEN 111
CHAPTER 57 ✠ SHINDARAS PLAN 131
CHAPTER 58 ✠ FRIENDS REUNITED 151
CHAPTER 59 ✠ RUBBED THE WRONG WAY 177

HE GAVE ME A MESSAGE...
"GOOD-BYE, YUYA-SAN."
SAMURAI DEEPER KYO
CHAPTER FIFTY-ONE - THE DEMON-BLADE MURAMASA
HE WON'T BE COMING BACK TO THE SURFACE.
WHAT?!

KYO!

WH-
WHAT'S
THAT
SUPPOSED
TO MEAN?!

WHAT
DOES HE
MEAN
"GOOD-
BYE"?!

KYO!
TELL
ME!

WHY...?

HOW COULD
YOU JUST SAY
GOOD BYE?

...WHAT IF I...
HUH?
WHAT WAS HE GOING TO SAY?
DON'T WORRY ...
YOU'LL MEET AGAIN. 'CAUSE SOON AS I FIND MY BODY, I'M GOING TO DRAG HIM OUT AND KILL HIM.
WHAT ...?
HAH HAH HA HA!
HAH HAH HAH!

OF COURSE, IF HIS SPIRIT'S ALREADY FADED, IT'LL BE TOO LATE.
HOW CAN YOU-- ARE YOU EVEN HUMAN?!
WHAT?!
ME? NO.
I'M DEMON EYES KYO, THE THOUSAND-SLAYER!
HA HA HA HA!
HOW CAN YOU SAY THAT?!
WHEN HE HESITATED JUST NOW...
HE WAS ON THE VERGE OF SAYING SOMETHING... BUT WHAT?!

GREETINGS... OR IS IT "LONG TIME NO SEE"?
....
KLAK
THERE WAS ONE AMONG THE TEN SHINOBI WHO STOOD WITH YUKIMURA AT IEYASU'S TOURNEY WHO WANTED TO KILL ME, BADLY. I COULD SENSE IT. IT WAS YOU, NO?
....
KLAK KLAK
SARUTOBI SASUKE... STRONGEST OF THE SANADA TEN.
....
KLAK
YEAH, I'VE HEARD THAT NAME BEFORE...
HIS FLUID MOVEMENTS MAKE HIM A GIFTED KILLER. AS POWERFUL AS YUKIMURA, AND AN ASSASSIN WHOSE CRUELTY KNOWS NO PEER.
KLAK
YOU'RE STILL A CHILD. YOU SHOULD TAKE IT EASY.

TAKE IT EASY YOURSELF...
...DEMON EYES KYO-SAN.
EH? YOU... CHALLENGING ME?
AH, THAT REMINDS ME.
YOU NEED ME.
YOU'LL NEVER GET INTO THE LAND OF THE FIRE LOTUS OTHERWISE.
KLIK
KLAK
WHAT DO YOU MEAN BY THAT?!
IT'S SIMPLE, REALLY.
THERE'S A SPECIAL PATH INTO THE LOTUS LAND.
YUKIMURA SENT ME TO GUIDE YOU.

BUT YUKIMURA-- HE TOLD ME I COULD CHOOSE WHETHER OR NOT TO TAKE THE ASSIGNMENT.
KLAK
AND I CHOOSE "NO."
IT'D TAKE A *GOOD* FIGHT TO CONVINCE ME OTHERWISE.
...
SA... SASUKE-SAN!
AW, HE WANTS IT TOO, YOU CAN TELL.
HE'S AS MUCH A PART OF THIS FOREST AS I AM!
DON'T TRY TO HIDE IT. THE SMELL GIVES YOU AWAY.
THAT STENCH OF THICK *FOREST-BORN* BLOOD YOU CAN'T GET RID OF.
...
KYO...
SO HE *WAS* BORN HERE!

THAT, AND I WANT TO ASK YOU ABOUT THAT "MURA-MASA."
C'MON, LET ME TEST YOU.
FINE. I'VE BEEN WANTING TO CUT THAT SMIRK OFF YOUR FACE.
WE'LL SEE HOW WELL YOUR BLADE CUTS AND WHETHER YOU'RE EVEN WORTH GUIDING!
EH?
W-WAIT! HEY! GUYS!
WHAT'RE YOU--

NEWS, MASTER ...
AJIRA TELLS US KYO HAS DEFEATED KUBIRA.

I SEE.
THE TWELVE HAVE LOST THE TWIN STARS OF MEKIRA AND KUBIRA...
NOW WE ARE TEN...
WE WILL STRIKE BACK. LET US PRE-PARE--
NO NEED. LEAVE THIS TO AJIRA.
BUT, MASTER! AJIRA--NO, AKIRA IS NOT TO BE TRUSTED!
HE WILL BETRAY YOU, MASTER.
BE CALM, BASARA.
THERE IS ONLY ONE WAY INTO THE LOTUS LAND, AND I'VE MADE PREPARATIONS TO STOP THEM THERE.
ALL ARE PAWNS IN MY HAND.
THEY CAN SQUIRM ALL THEY WANT, IT MEANS NOTHING.
BUT LOOK UP, BASARA...

OUR STARS SHINE EVEN BRIGHTER.
OUR TIME IS AT HAND.
DO YOU KNOW HOW LONG I HAVE WAITED FOR THIS, BASARA?
YES, MASTER!
AT LAST! THE TIME WHEN WE SHALL RULE THE WORLD IS NIGH!
THE WORLD SHALL ONCE MORE BE COVERED IN THE DARKNESS OF FEAR!
IT IS AS YOU SAY, MASTER.
HEH HEH HEH ...
HAH HA HA HA
HA HA!

ダンッ
ヒュオオオ

SAY, KYO...

DO YOU KNOW WHY A MURAMASA IS ALSO CALLED A "DEMON-BLADE"?

....

FASCINATING, ISN'T IT? YET MORE INTERESTING STILL IS THAT THOSE WHO WIELD THIS BLADE ALWAYS DIE UNTIMELY DEATHS.
A MURAMASA ALWAYS SEEKS A MASTER WHO WILL GIVE IT MORE BLOOD
PEOPLE THINK THE DEMON-BLADE WANTS TO KILL TOKUGAWA.
BUT THEY'RE WRONG. IT WANTS TO KILL EVERYBODY.
BUT SOME AMONG THE DEMON-BLADE MURAMASAS ARE PARTICULARLY SPIRITED.
THERE ARE FOUR DEMONS AMONG THE DEMON-BLADES IN THIS WORLD. ONLY FOUR.
AND OF THEM, ONE IS THE TENRO--THE "SKY-WOLF"--A GREAT SWORD, FIVE SHAKU LONG. ITS CUT AND CURVE ARE THINGS OF BEAUTY.
MANY SAMURAI DESIRED IT, BUT NONE COULD HOLD IT. FOR THE TENRO IS SAID TO HAVE DRUNKEN THE BLOOD OF TEN THOUSAND MEN!
NOW, WE HAVE A PROBLEM:
THERE ARE TWO MURAMASAS HERE: BOTH SEEM TO BE THE TENRO. ONE IS A FAKE.
....

SO, KYO-SAN...
LET'S FIND OUT!
OOF!
S-SA-SUKE-KUN! HE'S GONE?!

MINE!

I CAN'T TELL WHO WILL WIN!
I GUESS IT'S MY TURN...
driiip
...
WELL...
ザッ
NO. I YIELD.
WHAT?!
チャキッ
THE MYS-TERY'S SOLVED.

LOOKS LIKE MINE IS A PLAIN OLD MURAMASA.
OR I MIGHT TRY TO KILL YOU FOR REAL.
WHATEVER. YOU WERE HOLDING BACK.
I COULD SAY THE SAME TO YOU. AND HERE I THOUGHT YOU WERE STILL RECOVERING...
H-HIS SWORD! IT CRACKED!
AND YOU'VE SHOWN YOU CAN FIGHT. BEST STOP NOW.
YOU'RE THE FIRST PERSON I'VE MET IN A WHILE WHO'S WORTH KILLING.
ANYTIME YOU LIKE. ANYTIME.

SNIK
YOU PASSED THE TEST.
I'LL BE YOUR GUIDE.
KYU–
TO THE ICE FORTRESS, IN THE LAND OF THE FIRE LOTUS!
Clack

上条事情 Kamijyo Circumstances

☒ AYU

And... there were no votes for Bikara.

To you who sent the only vote for Bikara, you who supported me these past seven years but are too courteous to think of bragging about it, thank you!

◉ Yo! Kamijyo here. Now, I like doing these bonus pages for you. I'd like to put in so many, you could open this here manga to any page and find one! Got to give you your money's worth, right? Still, this is the seventh volume, and I'm not quite used to doing these yet. Ach! My brain hurts. (Not that doing the manga itself is easy, mind you.)

Let's talk about the favorite character poll. Thanks for all the postcards! The cards written with passion, the cards with cool drawings, the piles of cards sent in by the same people :-)... I figure this is my only chance to hear your voices, and believe me, it's been educational. The top characters had some obvious winners, and some that were a big surprise. What did you think?

For me, Kubira was the big surprise--he got 10th place through sheer volume of votes. Sasuke showed up just as we started the poll, so his results were so-so. But the other characters are happy for your support! Thanks so much.

SAMURAI DEEPER
KYO
CHAPTER FIFTY-TWO -
VISITOR ON A DARK NIGHT

IT'S NO GOOD...

I'VE PRETTY MUCH FIGURED OUT KYO WAS BORN HERE.

KYO? ARE YOU LISTENING?
KYO ...?
ZZZZ... ZZZ...
KYO ...
HE'S ASLEEP... BUT HE NORMALLY WAKES UP AT THE SLIGHTEST NOISE.
THE FIGHT WITH KUBIRA MUST HAVE DRAINED HIM...
I'LL LET HIM SLEEP. HE WOULDN'T TELL ME ANYTHING IF HE WERE AWAKE, ANYWAY.
BUT...
YOU'RE KYO-SHIRO!
KYOSHIRO...
HE WOULDN'T TELL ME ANYTHING EITHER.

IS IT BECAUSE OF SAKUYA-SAN THAT HE WON'T COME OUT?

SAKUYA-SAN...THE ONLY WOMAN KYO LOVES.

WHAT KIND OF WOMAN IS SHE?

WHAT HAPPENED BETWEEN THE THREE OF THEM?

CAN'T SLEEP NE-CHAN?

I...I JUST HAVE SOME-THING ON MY MIND.
OKAY ...
I WONDER WHERE SAKUYA-SAN IS NOW?
SIGH
......
SASUKE... CAN YOU DO ME A FAVOR?
WHAT?
HOPE IT'S NOTHING TOO ANNOYING.
Not at all! ♡
Not at all! ♡
YOU KNOW HOW SAKUYA-SAN IS HERE?
SHHH....
JUST... DON'T TELL ANYONE IN THE FOREST, PLEASE?
WHY?
IT'S COMPLI-CATED. I'LL HOLD YOU TO IT.
....
YOU'LL MEET HER BEFORE LONG. IF YOU'RE STILL ALIVE.

I WOULD LIKE TO MEET SAKUYA SAN.
I... I GUESS.
I WONDER WHAT WOULD HAPPEN IF WE MET HER.
WHAT WOULD KYOSHIRO AND KYO DO?
YOU SHOULD GET TO SLEEP YOU'LL NEED IT WHEN WE GET CLOSER TO THE LOTUS LAND.
I'M ON WATCH, OKAY?
KLIK
.... THANKS, SASUKE-KUN!
AWH...SO SWEET! I WONDER IF YOU'LL BE SO SWEET TO ME!
WH- WHO'S THERE?!
DEAD ASLEEP IN THE FOREST?
KYO MUST BE QUITE CONFIDENT!
KLOK
WH... WHO...

HOW... MANLY! I THINK I'M IN LOVE. ♡
BIKARA !!!
WHY ARE YOU HERE?
HEE HEE ♡ WHY, ISN'T IT OBVIOUS?
I CAME TO KILL KYO. ♡
ニヤァ
...
NOOO, ACTUALLY, I'M JUST LOST IN THE WOODS!
Where'd Shindara and Antera go...?
BUT TO THINK I'D RUN INTO KYO! IT MUST BE THE POWER OF LOVE!
EEK?!
...
HOW COULD ONE SO BLATANTLY IDIOTIC GET SO CLOSE WITHOUT ME NOTICING?

WELL NOW...
IT'S NICE TO MEET KYO AND ALL, BUT SEEING AS HOW HE'S ASLEEP...
...
OH, DO I STARTL YOU? YES, I MA BE STRONG, BUT I AM FAR TOO GENTLE TO RUDEL AND SAVAGELY WAKE A SLEEPIN SAMURAI.
HEE HEE
OOH...
AAH!
!?
AAAH!
AAA...
AAAAAAAH!
JUST A SCRATCH
A...A CUT UPON MY...MY BEAUTIFUL, STRONG, FACE!

HOW COULD YOU?! MY... MY CULTIVATED SKIN!
I don't believe it!
IS THIS GUY REALLY TOUGH?
OR JUST... A FREAK.
WHAT DID YOU SAY TO ME?!
NOBODY CALLS ME A FREAK!
THAT ...
THAT IS IT!!!

NICE TRY.
はっ
NOW.
TIME FOR YOUR SPANKING, YOU BAD LITTLE BOY. ♡

BEAUTY! LOVE!
AND VIOLENCE! BIKARA-STYLE!
SA... SASUKE-KUN!
OH MY...
YOU'RE NOT JUST A KID, I SEE.
Nice utsusemi!
ZUP ZUP
AND YOU'RE NOT JUST A FREAK.
PHEW! HE'S OKAY!

THIS BIG GUY IS ONE OF THE TWELVE, AFTER ALL.
NICE TRICKSIES, BOY. I LOVE FASHIONABLE LADS LIKE YOU ♡
HEE HEE!♡
KLIK
THE WAY HE MOVED, HIS STRENGTH-- THEY'RE OFF THE CHARTS!
WOULD KY BE ABLE T BEAT HIM NOW?
HOW EVER.
はっ
I HATE PRETTY GIRLS.
Especially ones that make fun of me.
IT'S NO FAIR!!!
EASY LIFE, NEVER HAVE TO DO ANY-THING BUT BE CUTE...
NE... NE-CHAN!
I'M TOO LATE!
AAAAAH!

HOW AM I SUPPOSED TO SLEEP WITH THAT ON?
IT'S YOUR FAULT. THIS BLANKET'S TOO HOT.
K... KYO...
AWAKE AT LAST! YOU SURE MADE ME WAIT! PLAYING HARD TO GET, HUH? ♡
YOU'RE PERSIS-TENT, AS ALWAYS.
HEE HEE YOU THINK SO?
...

BUT I'VE WAITED SO LONG
IT'S BEEN FOUR YEARS.
...
huff
haah
huff
huff
gasp

NOW THIS IS FUN! HOW LONG HAVE WE BEEN FIGHTING HERE?
huff
huff
QUITE A WHILE, EH?
Five, six hours?
Drip
huff

MORE FUN YET TO COME!
I'M READY.

WE FOUGHT A WHOLE DAY AFTER THAT WITH NO WINNER!
WELL... SHALL WE DANCE TONIGHT?
JUST US TWO. ♡ A DANCE TO THE DEATH!
HOW COULD I REFUSE?
HE FOUGHT A WHOLE DAY WITH DEMON EYES KYO?!
...
HOW STRONG COULD HE BE...?
KYO STILL HASN'T HEALED FROM HIS FIGHT WITH KUBIRA!
gulp
BUT WAIT...
KYO... YOU CAN'T WIN!!!

KYO-HAAAAN! YUYA-HAAAAN!
ガラ
WHERE ARE YOU?
ガラ
HURRY UP AND FIND THEM, TORA-SAN
I TIRE OF BEING ALONE WITH YOU.
ガラ
sigh...
...
OKUNI-HAN! YOU COULD HELP, TOO, Y'KNOW!
WELL! AND YOU CALL YOURSELF A MAN?!
I HATE HER. I HATE HER.
IT'S A SHAME REALLY
WHEN WE FOUND THEM, I WAS GOING TO TELL YUYA-SAN HOW WONDERFUL YOU WERE...
TIRED? ME? NEVER!
I'll find 'em quick! Just tell them how great I was, okay?
SO SIMPLE...
Of course.

ガラ ガラ
YUYA-HAN'S GONNA DIG ME! ♡
A wedding in June...got to pick a lucky day!
!
WH...
WHO'S THERE?!
...MY MY.
WHAT HAVE WE HERE?
snicker
Y... YOU!
HOW DID YOU GET SO CLOSE?! I DIDN'T SENSE ANYTHING!

AKIRA...
HERE, IN THE MIDDLE OF AOKIGAHARA, UTTERLY **HEEDLESS** OF YOUR SURROUNDINGS. IT'S SO FUNNY, IT'S SAD.
AND NO KYO TO GUARD YOU?
THINGS JUST DIDN'T WORK OUT, AND HE DITCHED YOU. AM I RIGHT?
AKIRAAAA!!
OH? A CHALLENGE? VERY WELL.
BUT ALLOW ME TO SAY ONE THING...

I'M NOT HOLDING BACK.
NOT ANYMORE.
YEAH...
IT'S ABOUT TIME!!!

CHAPTER FIFTY-THREE - THE BIGGEST DUMMY IN THE WORLD

AKIRA-HAN... YOU GOT LUCKY THE OTHER DAY, BUT DON'T GET CARRIED AWAY.
`CAUSE NOW IT'S PAY-BACK TIME.
...
YOU CAN JOIN MEKIRA IN THE TRASH HEAP.
BUT YOUR SISSY FIGHTING STYLE'S THE BIGGEST JOKE OF ALL!
ZZZUP
AH... ALWAYS WITH THE HUMOR.
YEAH ...
REALLY? WHAT A PITY.
...
TORA-SAN DID DEFEAT MEKIRA, ONE OF THE TWELVE...
クス
IF ONLY THE DEAD COULD LAUGH.
BUT AKIRA'S ONE OF THE FOUR EMPERORS... HE'S AS STRONG AS KYO!
AND TORA TOOK A HIT IN HIS RIBS AND HIS LEFT LEG AGAINST MEKIRA!

HOW CAN HE FIGHT AKIRA WOUNDED?!

GRR!
YAAAH!

MINE!
TORA-SAN GOT HIS BACK!
IT'S OVER!
AKIRAAAA!

...
?!
WHA... WHAT'S WRONG, TORA?

HMM? WHAT HAPPENED? THAT WAS YOUR CHANCE.

ONE MORE STEP...

I WAS ONE STEP AWAY... WHEN THAT HATRED HIT ME! WHAT WAS THAT?!

THIS ISN'T GOING TO BE EASY.

TIME TO BREAK OUT THE TRICKS

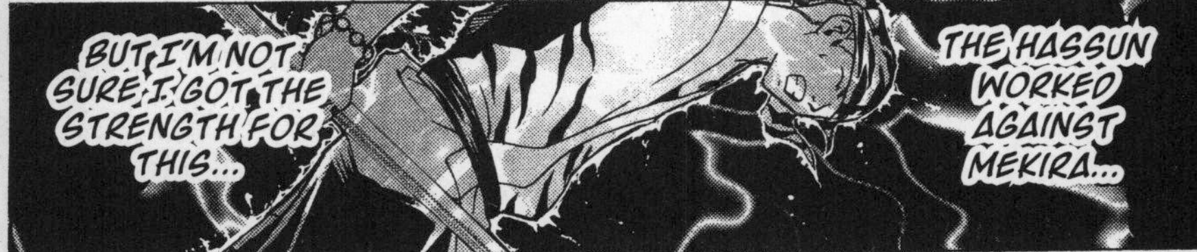

PERHAPS YOU'VE FINALLY REALIZED? NO MATTER HOW HARD YOU TRY, THERE WILL ALWAYS BE **THREE GAPS** BETWEEN YOU AND ME.
THE FIRST IS **EXPERIENCE.** I'VE FOUGHT ON THE BATTLEFIELD SINCE I WAS TEN. I CAN REACT FASTER THAN YOU.
THE SECOND IS **TECHNIQUE.** I'VE HAD TO LEARN MORE WAYS TO KILL PEOPLE TO SURVIVE.
AND FINALLY ...
THE THIRD IS A GAP OF CONVICTION.
I FIGHT WITH MY LIFE. YOU, YOU SPOILED TOKUGAWA BRAT, FIGHT FOR FUN.
I STILL CAN'T BELIEVE YOU'RE **ALLOWED** TO STAND NEXT TO KYO.
.....
TORA-SAN..
NOW'S YOUR CHANCE TO RUN, **BRAT.**
IT'S NOT TOO LATE. GO BACK AND LEECH OFF DADDY.
WHY NOT GO DREAM OF RULING THE WORLD, TOKUGAWA HIDETADA, HMM?
THAT BLOOD-SOAKED FAMILY TREE SUITS YOU WELL.

WHY?
ANSWER ME, FATHER!
WHY ARE YOU LEAVING TORII TO DIE?! HE'S YOUR FRIEND!
YOU GOTTA SACRIFICE YOUR RETAINER JUST TO WIN THIS BATTLE?
WHY, FATHER?!
LISTEN TO ME, HIDETAD
BY SACRIFICING TORII, I CAN END THE BATTLE WITH TOYOTOMI THAT MUCH SOONER AND SAVE THE LIVES OF TENS OF THOUSANDS OF OUR PEOPLE.
REMEMBER THAT! THAT IS WHAT IT MEANS TO RULE THE WORLD!
I GUESS SO.
THAT'S WHAT I MUST LOOK LIKE TO YOU.
BUT, YOU KNOW WHAT?

I'M NOT SMART ENOUGH TO SACRIFICE A FEW TO SAVE MANY...
YOU KNOW?
I DON'T CARE IF PEOPLE CALL ME STUPID.
I PROTECT MY FRIENDS!
TORA-SAN...
THE EXCUSE OF A WEAKLING WHO CANNOT LEAD.
YEAH... YEAH...
THAT'S RIGHT...
THAT'S WHY I GOTTA GET STRONGER!

HE... HE'S FAST!
YOU DIE HERE.
TORA-SAN!
NO! HE'LL BE KILLED!
STUPID I MAY BE...
BUT ...

I'M NOT YOUR AVERAGE DUMMY!

GAH!

ON SECOND THOUGHT, I'LL LET YOU LIVE A LITTLE LONGER.
EH ...?!
WH... WHAT'YA MEAN?!
AH-HA, NO NEED TO PANIC!
THIS BENITORA...
HIS EXPERIENCE, TECHNIQUE, CONVICTION... THESE ARE JOKES.
BUT JUST NOW...
THE ANIMOSITY I FELT FROM HIM.
IT WAS GREATER THAN MINE. IT STOPPED MY SWORD.
I CAN USE HIM.
LET ME REPAY YOU FOR THE ENTERTAINMENT.
HUH?
I'LL TELL YOU THAT WHICH THE TOKUGAWA MOST WANT TO KNOW...

THE IDENTITY OF THE MASTER!
HUH?!

YAAH!

ざっ
ちゃき

......
NOT LIKE YOU TO FIGHT QUIETLY.
OR IS THIS A NEW STYLE? BELIEVE ME, IT'S A CHANGE FOR THE BETTER.
BIKARA DOESN'T EVEN HAVE ROOM TO CRACK A SMILE!
KYO ...!
KYO HAS HIM RUNNING!
IF HE CAN KEEP IT UP, KYO WILL WIN!
...

THINGS DON'T LOOK GOOD FOR DEMON EYES.
KLOK
WHAT?!
KYO HAS HIM CORNERED, AND IT HASN' EVEN BEEN FIVE MINUTES!
DEMON EYES KYO WILL LOSE. I'LL BET YOU ON IT.
...
KLAK
EH...?
WHAT ARE YOU TALKING ABOUT, SASUKE-KUN?
...

I'M SAYING THAT IF THIS GOES ON, THAT BRUTE WILL KILL DEMON EYES KYO.
KYO...DEMON EYES KYO... WILL LOSE?
WHAT ?!

THAT FIVE-SHAKU SWORD...
WITH IT, HE'S KILLED A THOUSAND MEN. HE'S WON A THOUSAND BATTLES.
THE LEGENDARY KYO... LOSE?
SAMURAI DEEPER KYO

DEFEAT?!
SAMURAI DEEPER
KYO
CHAPTER FIFTY-FOUR
DEMON EYES' DEFEAT

HRAH!

K... KYO!!!
BIKARA...
AS STRONG AS YOU ARE, IF YOU NEVER HIT ME, YOU CAN NEVER WIN.
STILL CLAMMED UP? IT'S NOT LIKE YOU!
Lunch not agreeing with you?
....
KYO'S FINE!
I KNEW KYO COULDN'T LOSE!
RIGHT, SASUKE-KUN? BIKARA MAY BE STRONG, BUT HE HASN'T HIT KYO ONCE!
HE CAN'T BEAT KYO WITH STRENGTH ALONE!
HE'S HITTING AIR!
....

...EH?
PEH
IT'S NO GOOD.
WHAT'S WRONG? COME AND GET ME! LOSE YOUR WILL TO FIGHT?
...
TELL ME...
WHERE IS THE REAL DEMON EYES KYO?
?!
YOU'RE NOT THE KYO I FOUGHT ON THE BLOOD-DRENCHED FIELDS...
THE KYO WHO GAVE ME SUCH PLEASURE WAS STRONG, GRACEFUL...
THAT KYO IS THE TRUE KYO.
MY HEART BEATS FOR HIM ALONE!
...

WHERE IS HE? WHERE?!
SNIFF
はら はら
WHAT?
...
YOU'VE BROKEN THIS GENTLE MAIDEN'S HEART...
AND YOU'LL PAY!!!
WHAT DOES HE MEAN? HOW IS KYO WEAK?
HE MAY BE TIRED, BUT HE'S DODG-ING FINE, AND HE'S STILL GOT TIME LEFT!
SNIFF

I MISREAD HIM MYSELF.
WH
BIKARA. YOU'D THINK FROM HIS MUSCLES, TEMPERAMENT, AND CHOICE OF WEAPON THAT HE WAS ONE TO WIN BY *SHEER STRENGTH*.
BUT THAT'S A *BIG* MISTAKE.
HE'S STRONG, YES...
BUT HE CAN ALSO READ AN OPPONENT. AND THAT WEAPON OF HIS IS FOR SHOW.
SEE, HE'S A *HAND-TO-HAND* SPECIALIST.
OH, AND...
HE' GOT ONE MOR TRIC
YOU!
BEAUTY! LOVE!
VIOLENCE! BIKARA STYLE!
IF I HAD REALIZED IT ONE SEC-OND LATER, IT WOULD HAVE BEEN TOO LATE.
THAT CUT ...

SPEED. THAT'S HIS GREATEST WEAPON.
EVEN I, ONE OF THE TEN, COULDN'T DODGE HIM ENTIRELY
HE'S FASTER THAN ME, THAT'S FOR SURE.
...
HIS GREATEST WEAPON...?
HERE I COME, BIG BOY!
I'LL GIVE YOU 50% SPEED FOR STARTERS!
♡
GUH ...!
YOU MEAN THAT BEHEMOTH IS MORE FAST THAN STRONG?!

SLOW!
DAMN!
KYO ...!
THE OLD KYO WOULD HAVE LAUGHED THAT OFF!
YOU'RE NO DEMON EYES!
And hit back!
...
I THINK I'LL JUST KILL YOU NOW THIS IS TOO DEPRESS-ING.

80%! THAT SHOULD BE MORE THAN ENOUGH FOR YOU!
HE'S TOO FAST TO SEE!
?!
DAMN ...!
K... KYO...!
DEMON EYES KYO CAN'T KEEP UP.
THE SPEED WEAVES A TRAP, AND IF HE FALLS IN, BIKARA'S POWER AND BLADES WILL DICE HIM.

KYO!
GWUH!
YOU'RE SO SLOW IT'S PAINFUL. A FLY COULD LAY EGGS ON YOU!
THIS IS THE END.
BYE BYE, KYO-SAN.
IT'S OVER.

BEAUTY! POWER! THE BIKARA VICTORY SMASH!

NO...
NO!!!

WHAT?!
ARE YOU CRAZY?!
HEY!
YOU'RE DUMBER THAN ME!
YOU EXPECT ME TO BELIEVE HE'S THE MASTER?!
BUT... BUT...!
BELIEVE IT OR NOT. IT'S YOUR CHOICE.

BUT THE TRUTH IS THE TRUTH.
IT CAN'T BE... IF THAT'S TRUE...
THE MASTER IS ALIVE.
THEN THE WORLD WILL FALL INTO DARKNESS. THE RIVERS WILL RUN RED!
...
YOU CAN'T JUST STAND BY, CAN YOU?
YOU'RE A TOKUGAWA. IT'S IN YOUR BLOOD.
NAH. THE TOKUGAWA HOUSE THREW ME OUT A WHILE AGO.
I DON'T CARE WHO RULES THE WORLD. STILL...
EVEN IF THE WORLD DOES GO TO HELL...
...THERE'S ONE THING I'LL DO.

I'LL PROTECT YUYA-HAN, COME WHAT MAY!

THAT'S ALL!

SO, AKIRA-HAN, WHY *DID* YOU TELL ME?

WE'RE ENEMIES, RIGHT? WHAT ARE YOU UP TO?

....!
I AM NO ONE'S ALLY. I SEEK NO ONE'S AID.
IT'S SIMPLE ....
I LIVE FOR THAT ONE PURPOSE ALONE.
AND I PLAN TO DIE FOR THAT ONE PURPOSE.
W... WAIT!
THAT'S NOT A STRAIGHT ANSWER!
BENITORA-SAN...
WEREN'T YOU JUST SAYING YOU'D PROTECT YUYA-SAN?
?!
IF THAT'S SO...
I HAVE ONE GOAL: TO KILL HE WHO GAVE ME EVERYTHING AND TOOK IT ALL AWAY.
TO KILL DEMON EYES KYO.

THEN YOU SHOULD GO TO HER SIDE. FAST.
WHAT ?!
I'M RATHER FOND OF HER, TOO, YOU KNOW. SO GENTLE, YET SPIRITED.
IT'S TOO EARLY...
...FOR HER TO DIE.
WHY, YOU--!
THAT GIRL IS FAST BECOMING KYO'S WEAKNESS. THE MASTER WILL TAKE ADVANTAGE OF THAT.
And everyone else after kyo.
IT HAPPENS TO EVERY WOMAN NEAR HIM.
NO EXCEPTIONS.

NO...
WHA DID H MEAN
IT COULDN'T BE... NO!
NOT YUYA-HAN!
ARRGGH!
OKUNI-HAN! GET ON!
WE GOTTA FIND YUYA-HAN!
C-COMING!
TSK
WHAT'S GOING TO HAPPEN TO YUYA-HAN?!
I'M NOT LEAVING HER SIDE AGAIN! EVER!
KYO-HAN! I HOPE YOU'RE WITH HER!

KEEP HER SAFE TILL I GET THERE! PLEASE!!!
YOU'RE STRONG, KYO.
KYO!
PROTECT HER!

LET'S ALL FOLLOW THE LAW, SHALL WE?
ALL AT ONCE!
THE STRONG ARE STRONG...
...AND THE WEAK ARE DEAD.
ONCE MORE... C'MON
WHAT'S WRONG?
C'MON!!
STAY CLOSE.
WHAT'S WRONG?
NOT HAPPY TO SEE ME?
KYO...
SAMURAI DEEPER KYO

KYOOOOOOO!!!

...

SIGH... SO... ANTI-CLIMACTIC.
IT'S SAD, REALLY. TO BEAT THE MIGHTY KYO-SAN SO EASILY...

STILL ...
I'M SURE THE MASTER WILL BE HAPPY.
I DON'T BELIEVE IT!
KYO'S NOT DEFEATED! HE CAN'T BE! KYO...KYO NEVER LOSES!

SAMURAI DEEPER KYO
CHAPTER FIFTY-FIVE - THE DEMONS' HEARTBE
ALWAY ...
ALWAYS ...
ALWAYS!
KYO ALWAYS LAUGHS AT HIS ENEMIES.
AND... AND...
HE'S ALWAYS SO SURE OF HIMSELF!
HE ALWAYS STANDS THERE, IN FRONT OF ME.

AND THEN HE SMILES...
WELL... YOU LOOK LIKE A DOG PUKED.
I BELIEVE IN YOU, KYO!
SO GET UP! STAND! IGHT!!!
THAT'S WHY I CAN'T STAND WOMEN.
ホウ
SO MOTIONAL!
ギロ
AND YOU CAN STOP WITH THE "KYO, KYO"...
THIS EAKLING OESN'T ESERVE HE NAME F DEMON EYES!

WATCH YOUR MOUTH!
Um, ne-chan?
KYO IS STRONG! HE COULD NEVER LOSE TO A FREAK LIKE YOU!
LOOK IN THE MIRROR BEFORE YOU CAL KYO NAMES!
ピク
YOU BIG FREAK!
WHAT ARE YOU? HARD OF HEARING? FREAK! FREAK!!! FREAK!!!
EVEN I COULD BEAT A FREAK LIKE YOU!
WH... ...DID YO SAY?
AND WA GOIN TO B NICE
HUH?
KILLING YOU DIDN'T LOOK LIKE MUCH FUN, SEE?
SO I WAS GOING TO SPARE YOUR LIVES.
BUT YOU'VE INSULTED ME.
AND NOW... YOU DIE!
I hate that word! And you said it a lot!

DIE DIE DIE!
AAAAAAH!
YOU WANT SOME TOO BOY?
KRIK KRAK
THIS NE-CHAN'S UNDER MY PROTECTION.
I'M NDER STRICT RDERS FROM YUKIMURA.

CUTE LITTL BOY. ♡ WANTS TO B A MAN.
OKAY.
I'LL SHOW YOU HOW TO BE A MAN! ♡
OH, NO! SASUKE-KUN...!
HOW CAN HE BEAT SOMEONE WHO DEFEATED KYO?!
...

ON SECOND THOUGHT, I PASS.
WHAT ?!
SMART BOY! ♡
PART OF BEING STRONG IS KNOWING WHEN YOU'RE BEAT.
GOOD BOY! WE CAN FIGHT WHEN YOU GROW UP. I'LL BE WAITING! ♡
Grow up nice and strong, eh?
NOW. STEP ASIDE.
YOU CAN GO...
BUT NOT HER! I'M GOING TO RIP HER UP AND THROW A PIECE UNDER EVERY TREE IN THIS FOREST!
....
KLIK
....
YOU MISUNDERSTOOD ME...
WHAT ...?

I STEPPED DOWN...
I DIDN'T STEP DOWN BECAUSE I'M A "BOY."
...BECAUSE YOU'RE NOT FINISHED.

KYO?!
KYO!!!
...
WELL NOW, THIS IS A SURPRISE! YOU SURVIVED MY CRUSHER?
HNN?

...
... KYO
WHY... WHY DOESN'T HE SAY ANYTHING ?
WAIT... MAYBE ...?!
YOU'RE KYO-SHIRO!
MAYBE ...IT'S JUST LIKE BEFORE!
KYOSHIRO'S COME BACK?!
COME ON! WHAT HAPPENED TO THE USUAL BANTER, EH?
...
TALK! THIS ISN'T FUN AT ALL!
grumble grumble
IF YOU'RE NOT GOING TO BE ENTER-TAINING...

...THEN YOU CAN DIE!
KYO !!!
BIKARA IS TOO FAST FOR HIM!
...
NO, YOU'RE WRONG.
WHAT?

LET'S END THIS. YOU CAN LAMENT YOUR LACK OF SPEE IN HELL!
...
NO LAS WORDS
OR NO BREATH WITH WHICH TO SPEAK THEM?
WELL.
I'VE WAITED LONG ENOUGH!
NOOOOO!!!

WHA--?!
HE... HE'S GONE!
BUT WHERE ...?

GWAH!
K-KYO! HE DID IT!
YOU, FASTER THAN ME! HOW?!
HAA ...
KYO? WHAT ARE YOU?

...HEH HEH...
HEH HEH HEH ...
KYO ...?!
HEH HEH HEH ...
HEH HEH...
...HAH.
HAAAAAH!!! HAH HAH HAH HAH!

HA
YOU CAN'T FOOL SOMEO EVERY TIME WITH THE SAME TRICK.
BUT I SHOULD THANK YOU... SEE, YOU JOGGED MY MEMORY.
K...KYO? IS THAT YOU? BUT... SOMETHING FEELS DIFFERENT-- THAT POWER
I REMEMBE THIS BOD
AND... THAT SCAR ON HIS BACK. THE CRIMSON CROSS... IT'S SO CLEAR IT'S ALMOST GLOWING!
I REMEMBER... ...HOW TO FIGHT!
NOW...

LET ME
REMIND
YOU...

...WHAT IT IS TO FEAR DEMON EYES KYO.

I DON'T GET IT. HE WAS ON THE BRINK OF DEATH-- HE COULD BARELY STAND!
NOW HIS EYES SHINE WITH VIOLENCE!
...
...
K... KYO!
YOU'RE SCARING ME...
HE'S STILL KYO...BUT THE ANIMOSITY I FEEL IS A HUNDREDFOLD!
LIKE TALONS... GRIPPING MY HEART!
THE THOUSAND-KILLER... THE LEGEND...
THIS IS DEMON EYES KYO!

I'VE WAITED FOUR LONG YEARS.
HEH HEH... NOW IT'S GETTING INTERESTING!
I'VE BEEN WAITING TO FIGHT...
WELL, LET'S GET ON WITH IT.
BIKARA!
I'VE BEEN WAITING TO FIGHT YOU!

HEY! COME AND GET SOME!
SAMURAI DEEPER KYO
CHAPTER FIFTY-SIX
DEMON EYES OPEN

AW... WHAT'S WRONG? DON'T TELL ME YOU'RE SCARED!
...
YOU THINK I'M SCARED?
...FOOL.
I'VE BEEN WAITING FOR THIS, TOO.
WAITING ...
...TO FINISH WHAT WE STARTED!
I'LL CUT YOU DOWN TO SIZE!

YOU COULDN'T KILL A PUPPY WITH THESE.
DON'T BORE ME, PLEASE...
EH?!
YOU... CAUGHT THEM?!
'CAUSE THEN I MIGHT HAVE TO KILL YOU.
HOW LONG YOU GOING TO STAND THERE IN SHOCK?

GRR ...
YOU CALL THAT SUPERNATURAL STRENGTH? YOU DISAPPOINT ME!
UNF!
GWAH
HE... HE'S TOO STRONG!
NFAH!
HELLO! THE FIGHT'S OVER THIS WAY.
GRAAH!

WHAT? NOT HITTING BACK TODAY?
WHERE'S THE FUN IN KILLING YOU LIKE THIS?
GUH...
SO MUCH FASTER... THAN BEFORE!
MUCH FASTER THAN FOUR YEARS AGO!
YOU LOOK GOOD IN RED! HAH HAH!
HMM...
YOU WANT FUN?
I'LL GIVE YOU FUN!
TRY TO KEEP UP WITH 80% SPEED!

THAT'S NOT SPEED.
THIS IS SPEED.
?!
HE DISA--
HA-- ?!
THIS CAN'T BE!
HE'S FASTER THAN ME?!

HE'S FASTER THAN ME AT 100%?!
NRRAAH! YOU THINK I'M GOING TO STAND BY AND--
NO! I THINK YOU'RE GOING TO DIE.
HOW ...?

DID YOU REALLY BELIEVE ...
GUH!
NO...
GWUH!
GUH!
GAH!
...CAN'T BLOCK!
GUH!
...YOU COULD BEAT ME?

NOT IN A HUNDRED THOUSAND YEARS!

GWAAAAAH!
HAAAAH! HAH HAH HAH HA!
...HEH HEH...

YEAH... HE'S GOT A **WILD** LOOK IN HIS EYES.

HE WON'T STOP TILL BIKARA'S DEAD.

KLIK

WHAT ...?

NO. I'D SAY HE'S **DEADLY** SERIOUS.

BUT.. BIKARA--HE'S NOT...

...HE'S NOT JUST PLAYING, IS HE?

Sizing up the competition?

KYO IS TOO STRONG FOR HIM.

TO THINK THAT EMOTI COULD GET T DEMON EYE FIGHTING SPIRIT UP A GOING LIKE THIS.
EMOTION?
Interesting....
I THINK I'VE FIGURED IT OUT.
IT TAKES A REAL THREAT TO BRING OUT THE REAL KYO.
SO THIS IS HIM...
THIS KILLER...
THIS IS THE REA DEMON EYES KYO!
HAH HA HA! YOU CALL THIS A FIGHT?!
SASUKE ...?
KLAK
KLIK
SASUKE-KUN?!
KLOK
YUKIMURA'S GOT A CRUEL STREAK.

MAKING ME PLAY GUIDE WHEN THERE ARE SUCH INTERESTING PEOPLE TO FIGHT.
Maybe I should give up my day job...
SASUKE-KUN!
E'S ENJOYING THIS!
HE IS FROM THIS FOREST, AFTER ALL.
FEEL ICK O MY TOMACH, ND HE'S MILING!
NOW... THAT'S KYO!
YOU'RE BACK. ♡
READY TO DIE, YET?
PLEASE...
HY WOULD WANT TO ND ALL THIS FUN?

I'VE BEEN SAVING ANOTHER TRICK FOR YOU. ♡
!
SOMETHING ABOUT TO HAPPEN. HE DRAWING HIS KI BAC INSIDE HIM SELF...
THE NEXT BLOW WILL BE THE LAST!
OH? A TRICK, FOR ME?
Grit
IT BETTER BE A GOOD ONE.
!...
...KYO.
I'M A HARSH CRITIC!
YOU FORGET TO LOOK AROUND WHEN YOU'RE EXCITED...
Just like old times, eh?

BUT I WANT YOU TO SEE ME, KYO...
...AND HEAR ME.
THE GODS VON'T LOOK UT FOR YOU FOREVER, KYO.

IT'S SHINDARA! ONE OF THE TWELVE!
WATCH OUT, KYO!
THIS'LL BE GOOD.
クス
WELL? WHAT ARE YOU GO--
WHO DO YOU THINK YOU'RE TALKING TO?
ズズズ...
WHAT USE DO *DEMONS* HAVE FOR *GODS?*
You've left yourself open!

!!
GETTING CLOSE TO KYO NOW IS LIKE RACING TO YOUR OWN DEATH.
...
NICE THRUST.
I MUST APOLOGIZE...
BUT YOU CAN'T KILL ME LIKE THAT.

K-
KYO
...
I SEE YOU'RE AS IMMORTAL AS EVER.
WELL, SHIN-DARA...
PHEW
HE
OKA
BUT WHY?
KYO'S SWORD WENT RIGHT THROUGH SHINDARA... BUT HE LIVES!
What was that fire?
NOT AS UNKILLABLE AS YOU SEEM TO BE. POOR BIKARA!
BUT NEXT...
...YOU FACE ME.

DON'T HOLD BACK ON MY ACCOUNT.
I'LL TAKE YOU *BOTH* ON!
WHY KILL YOU ONE AT A TIME...
...WHEN I CAN KILL YOU *BOTH AT ONCE!*

AH, KYO...
YOU STILL HAVE A SENSE OF HUMOR.
ANY ONE O THE TWELVE YOUR EQUA THOUSAND- KILLER KYO
ANY ONE OF US POSSESSES POWER ENOUGH TO DESTROY THE WORLD.
AND YOU WOULD FIGHT TWO OF US?
YEAH, LIKE I SAID...
NO HOLDING BACK!
SAMURAI DEEPER KYO

CHAPTER FIFTY-SEVEN-
SHINDARA'S PLAN

HE CAN'T TAKE ON TWO OF THE TWELVE AT ONCE!
YES, HE'S STRONG-- TERRIBLY STRONG-- AND HE WAS WINNING AGAINST BIKARA...
BUT AGAINST SOMEONE HE AN'T CUT, WHO AKES FIRE OUT OF THIN AIR?!
KYO... CAN YOU REALLY WIN?
...
THE RUMORED SHINDARA, THE UNDYING.
SASUKE!
WAIT!
WAIT!

I FORGOT TO TELL YOU SOMETHING.
!?
WHAT? NOT AGAIN
THIS IS IMPORTANT, SO PAY ATTENTION. ♡
YOU'RE SURE TO MEET LOTS OF DANGEROUS PEOPLE IN THE FOREST. YOU SHOULD NEVER APPROACH THEM.
I know how you like danger.
MOST ESPECIALLY, YOU SHOULD AVOID ANY RUN-INS WITH THE TWELVE.
THERE'S BEEN A CHANGE IN THE GUAR SINCE SEKIGAHAR...
...BUT THEY USED TO HOLD THEIR OWN AGAINST KYO... THEY'RE STRONG!
THAT STRONG, EH?
YES, SA-SUKE.
STRONGER THAN YOU. ♡
I'll find 'em and kill 'em!
Ah... I was just kidding! ♡

IF YOU DO FIGHT, KEEP YOUR EYES OPEN. JUST...DON'T MAKE ME COME RESCUE YOU.
See, I trust you, Sasuke
ONLY...
...
WHATEVER YOU DO, DON'T FIGHT SHINDARA THE UNDYING.
NEVER!
WHAT? WHY?! YOU DON'T THINK I'D LOSE DO YOU?
THAT'S NOT IT...
HE'S GOT SOMETHING, SOMETHING MORE THAN STRENGTH...
UNDERSTOOD? WAIT... AT LEAST UNTIL I GET THERE.
...
YUKIMURA SPOKE HIGHLY OF YOU, SHINDARA...

WHAT'S THIS GUY'S SECRET?
HEY! HEY!!!
WHAT'S THE BIG IDEA?!
NO BUTTING SHINDARA
THIS IS A FIGHT BE-TWEEN ME AND KYO!
I WONDERED WHERE YOU'D GONE, BIKARA... SNEAKING OFF LIKE THAT!
Q-QUIET!!!
I'M FIGHTING KYO! GET IN MY WAY, AND I'LL KILL YOU, TOO, SHINDARA!
...
...

GOT IT? NOW GET GOING!

SAY THAT ONE MORE TIME...

WHO...

...WAS KILLING WHOM?

I NEVER DID LIKE THAT BIG MOUTH OF YOURS.

Or the face it's on.

Snap

Crackle

Crackle

Zap

THE POWER! I CAN'T BELIEVE BIKARA--OR SHINDARA, FOR THAT MATTER--STILL HAS IT IN HIM!
TWO OF THE TWELVE!
HAVE YOU FORGOTTEN?
HAVE YOU FORGOTTEN THE MASTER'S ORDERS?
ビクッ
Y-YEAH--I MEAN NO. TO FIND KYO'S BODY, RIGHT?
YES. PRECISELY.
SO WHAT ARE WE DOING HERE?
WELL... WHERE IS IT?
THAT'S WHY I'VE COME TO GET YOU.
ス
SEE, WE KNOW.

WE'VE FOUND THE ICE FORTRESS WHERE KYO'S BODY LIES!
OH NO!
KYO!

THEY'VE FOUND HIS BODY?!
SO YOU SEE, BIKARA WE'VE NO TIM TO BE PLAYIN AROUND HERE.
WE MUST MOVE FAST--
ヅッ

....
TELL ME!
TELL ME WHERE MY BODY IS NOW!!!
OR I'LL CUT YOU INTO LITTLE IMMORTAL PIECES!
....
NOW THAT WON'T DO.

BELIEVE ME, I WANT TO FIGHT YOU, BUT I'M SURE WE WOULD NOT EMERGE UNSCATHED, AND BESIDES THE MASTER'S ORDERS ARE FINAL.
NOW THAT WE KNOW WHERE YOUR BODY IS, WE MUST GO RETRIEVE IT.
IF YOU WON'T TELL ME
I'LL BEAT IT OUT OF YOU!
ONE MORE THING ...
KYO.
DON'T MOVE.
WHAT THE-- ?!

HOW DID THOSE GET THERE?
UFF!
I SOWED FIRESEEDS AROUND YOU A WHILE AGO.
HE ORE YOU OVE...
...THE MORE YOU BURN.
KYO ...!
OKAY, NOW I'M GETTING ANGRY!
EVEN KYO'S HARD-PRESSED... WE'D BETTER DO AS YUKIMURA SAID AND MAKE A BREAK FOR IT

NOW'S MY CHANCE! ♡
ぴょん ♡
DAMN! THERE WA
ONE MOR
ガキィ
KU
GA
SHE'S S-SO STRONG!
TEE HEE! ♡
にこっ
DAM--

AND A WIN FOR ANTERA-CHAN!
ARE YOU-
SASUKE-KUN!
AH...
WHO...?
HEE! ♡

HEH. IT'LL TAKE MORE THAN A FIREBALL TO STOP ME, SHINDARA.
WHO SAID ANYTHING ABOUT STOPPING YOU?
HUH? THEN WHAT DID YOU--
KYO...

KYO!!!
BASED ON OUR OBSERVATIONS, WE'VE DETERMINED THAT TAKING HER HOSTAGE WOULD BE QUITE EFFECTIVE.
THAT, AND IT SEEMS THERE ARE OTHERS IN THE FOREST, TOO, SO WE SHOULDN'T DALLY.
LET-ME GO!
WE'LL BE TAKING MISS YUYA-SAN WITH US.
OW! YOU'RE HURTING ME! LET GO!!!
IT GOES AGAINST EVEN MY STANDARDS TO DO SUCH A THING, BUT WE CAN'T HAVE YOU INTERFERING.

...
KYO, DON'T EVEN THINK ABOUT OPPOSING US.
UNLESS YOU WANT THIS GIRL TO DIE.
WE'LL BE STEALING YOUR BODY NOW, SO WAIT HERE.
I SAID LEMME GO!
Lemme--
はっ
KYO!

KYO!!!!

FIRST EVER

SDK DEEPEST-OF-THE-DEEP CHARACTER CONTEST RESULTS!

3rd Place:
Mibu Kyoshiro-- 3781 votes

4th Place:
Benitora--
2788 votes

5th Place:
Shiina Yuya--
2353 votes

2nd Place:
Sanada Yukimura -- 4584 votes

1st Place:
Demon Eyes Kyo-- 5256 votes

SAMURAI DEEPER KYO

CHAPTER FIFTY-EIGHT
FRIENDS REUNITED

8th Place:
Mahiro-- 245 votes

9th Place:
Shindara-- 196 votes

6th Place:
Akira-- 364 votes

7th Place:
Izumo-no-Okuni-- 297 votes

10th Place:
Kubira-- 136 votes

Big Thanks!

#17: Anayama Kosuke
#18: Shirokarasu (White Crow)
#19: Basara
#20: Mika's Father
#21: Mika
#22: Kamijyo
#23: Man with the Scar on his Back
#24: Mekira
#25: Fake Ieyasu
#26: Sasuke
#27: The Sanada Ten
#28: The Older Bantoji Brother
#29: Kurosasori (Black Scorpion)

OVER 20,543 VOTES RECEIVED! THANK YOU ALL SO MUCH!

KYO...
KYO, DON'T EVEN THINK ABOUT MOVING AGAINST US.
UNLESS YOU WANT TO SEE THIS GIRL DIE.
KYO ...
KYO!!!!

DAMMIT!
ズズズ..
THOSE BASTARDS WILL PAY!
NEVER HAVE I TASTED SUCH HUMILIATION!
ギッ
I'LL GET NE-CHAN BACK AND MAKE THEM REGRET THIS.
...
ぐ..

HMM ...
KYO-HAA-AAN!
WE LOOKED ALL OVER FOR YA!
THOUGHT WE'D NEVER SEE YOU AGAIN!
WOW! YOU'RE COVERED IN BLOOD--BUT YOU SEEM OKAY!
Sexy look, Kyo!
たったったっ
MAN, IT WAS HELL GETTING HERE!
SO, OKUNI-HAN! TELL THEM HOW GREAT I WAS!
C'mon!
...
AH! WAIT, BUT FIRST...
YUYA-HAN? WHERE'S YUYA-HAN?
キョロ キョロ
WHERE'S MY WELCOME BACK KISS?
...
GUYS...
WHERE'S YUYA?

ONEE-CHAN...
ONEECHAN...
HN?
HEY ONEE-CHAN!
WAKEY-WAKEY TIME!
WHERE AM I?
I MUST HAVE BEEN KNOCKED OUT WHEN THEY TOOK ME...
I'VE GOT A PRESENT FOR YOU, MISSY!
I MADE IT!
IT'S JUST FOR YOU! ♡
FLOWERS ...IN AOKIGAHARA?
おっ
HAT S THIS LACE ...?

A
FIELD OF
FLOWERS?

IT'S LIKE... HEAVEN!
DID WE LEAVE AOKIGAHARA FOREST?!
NO NO NO! WE'RE STILL IN THE FOREST. THIS IS THE SLOPE OF HELL!
WE HAVE TO GO THROUGH HERE TO GET TO KYO'S BODY, SEE.
C'MON! LET'S LOOK FOR A FOUR-LEAF CLOVER.
HOW CAN SUCH BEAUTY EXIST... HERE?
WAIT... COULD IT BE?
THERE'S A SPECIAL PATH INTO THE LOTUS LAND.
YUKIMURA SENT ME TO GUIDE YOU.
COULD THIS BE THE WAY SASUKE WAS TALKING ABOUT?
SAY, ONEE-CHAN? DON'T TRY TO ESCAPE, OKAY?
HUH ...?!
BIKARA'S, LIKE, TOTALLY WACKY RIGHT NOW.
NO TELLING WHAT HE MIGHT DO...
WHAT ARE YOU...
DON'T ELIEVE HIS!

WHY COULDN'T WE JUST KILL HIM?!
WHAT ARE WE, COWARDS?! YOU LISTENING TO ME, SHINDARA?!
THE MASTER SAYS THIS, THE MASTER SAYS THAT... WHAT ABOUT WHAT WE SAY? THE TWELVE?!
BIKARA, I KNOW YOU'RE UPSET.
I DON'T THINK THIS IS THE BEST WAY, EITHER.
...
CAN YOU BELIEVE IT HE'S BEEN LIKE THIS THE WHOLE TIME.
HOW-EVER.
SHIN-DARA...
NO WAY!
I'M AFRAID SO.

EEEK! YOU'RE BLEEDING!
SHINDARA'S BLEEDING!
KYO'S SWORD CUT!
HOW MANY YEARS HAS IT BEEN SINCE I'VE SEEN SHINDARA BLEED?
YOU OKAY? YOU OKAY?
YOU CAN'T BE DOING TOO WELL YOURSELF, BIKARA.
HRM...
TRUE, HAD WE KEPT FIGHTING, WE MIGHT NOT HAVE LOST.
PER-HAPS.
BUT THERE WAS NO GUARANTEE OF OUR VICTORY, EITHER.
....
I DON'T KNOW HOW, BUT DEMON EYES KYO IS STRONGER THAN HE WAS FOUR YEARS AGO.
IF HE GETS HIS HANDS ON HIS BODY, HIS POWER WILL BE UNFETTERED.
WE MUST FIND HIS BODY FIRST AND KEEP THAT FROM HAPPENING.
....
SHIINA YUYA-SAN?
MY APOLOGIES, UT YOU WILL BE ACCOM-PANYING US OR A WHILE.
EH?!

I DON'T WANT TO GET ROUGH, SO PLEASE, BE A GOOD GIRL.
ESPECIALLY HERE.
UNTIL WE PASS DOWN THE SLOPE OF HELL TO THE LOTUS LAND, WE ARE NOT SAFE.
THE SLOP OF HELL..
OH NO ...
YES.
THIS IS THE MOST BEAUTIFUL PLACE IN THE FOREST.
AND...
...THE MOST DEADLY
UNDER-STAND?
KYO...
WHERE ARE YOU?

WHY, KYO-HAN?!
WHY COULDN'T YOU PROTECT HER? YOU CALL YOURSELF A MAN?!
YOU JUST STOOD THERE AND WATCHED THEM TAKE HER AWAY?!
...
WELL? SAY SOMETHING!!!
I THOUGHT... I THOUGHT YOU'D PROTECT HER, KYO-HAN!
I BELIEVED IN YOU!
SO, WHY?!
YO- AN!!!
THEY CALL YOU THOUSAND-KILLER...
...AND YOU CAN'T EVEN SAVE A LITTLE GIRL?!

ばっ
KYO-HAN!
WAIT! YOU RUNNING AWAY? ANSWER M
TORA-SAN!
KYO HAN
I KNOW HOW YOU FEEL, BUT YOU CAN'T TAKE IT OUT ON KYO-SAN!
GRR...
I...I KNOW THERE'S SOME THINGS EVEN *KYO-HAN* CAN'T DO.
STILL ... STILL!
ARRGH! WHY?!
WHY DID I EVER LEAVE HER SIDE?!
WHAT DO I DO KNOW?
PLEASE, YUYA-HAN...
...DON'T LET THEM HURT YOU!

YOU SEEM DOWN!
UNUSUAL FOR YOU, KYO-SAN.

WHY ARE YOU HERE?
AH, COLD AS EVER, I SEE.

TO TEND TO YOUR WOUNDS, WHAT ELSE?
MOST PEOPLE WOULD BE GRATEFUL TO HAVE SUCH A BEAUTIFUL NURSE.
Show me that cut...

THAT'S A DEEP CUT! I'M SURPRISED YOU COULD STILL WALK!

MUST HAVE BEEN FRUSTRAT-ING...
...TO HAVE YOUR PUPPY DOG DRAGGED OFF BEFORE YOUR EYES.

HMM? YOU SHOULDN'T BE SURPRISED! I, IZUMO-NO-OKUNI, KNOW YOU BEST OF ALL!
YOU'RE MORE TORN ABOUT IT THAN HE IS...
BUT YOU'D NEVER LET IT SHOW. HOW SOCIALLY INEPT!
...
OF COURSE, THAT'S WHAT I LIKE ABOUT YOU!
HEE HEE ♡
...
SAY, KYO-SAN...
MAY I ASK YOU A QUES-TION?
THAT GIRL, SHIINA YUYA...
HOW IMPORTANT IS SHE TO YOU?
OR IS IT NOT HER AT ALL?

SHE JUST
LOOKS LIKE
SAKUYA-SAN!

OR LIKE SOMEONE ELSE?

FINISHED!

SORRY, BUT I'M HEADING OUT BY MYSELF.
NO TELLING WHAT'S HAPPENING TO YUYA-HAN WHILE WE SIT HERE.
GIVE IT UP.
THEY'RE EXPECTING YOU TO PANIC LIKE THIS.
WELL, IT'S BETTER THAN SITTING HERE DOING NOTHING!
WHAT DO YOU EXPECT TO ACCOMPLISH ALONE IN THE FOREST?
Not much, I bet.
!
LITTLE BRAT'S GOT A BIG MOUTH
LITTLE?
YEAH, YOU LITTLE PUNK. ISN'T MOMMY WAITING FOR YOU BACK ON KUDOYAMA?
SPOILED TOKUGAWA BONBON!
EVEN YOUR DADDY CAN'T HELP YOU IN AOKIGAHARA FOREST!
...
YOU'RE MAKING ME EXTREMELY ANGRY, YOU KNOW THAT?
I'll crush you, punk!
FUNNY, THE FEELING'S MUTUAL!
Try dying lately?

KYO-SAN... SHOULDN'T YOU STOP THEM?
KYO-SA--!
は
KYO-SAN ...?
HERE I COME!
!
?

!?
WHAZ ZAT?
That reeks!
SAKE ?!
WHAT THE HELL ...?
THAT SHOULD COOL YOU TWO OFF.

YUYA-SAN WOULDN'T APPROVE OF YOU FIGHTING.
EH, TORA-SAN?
YOU ...
HAVEN'T I TOLD YOU TO CONTROL YOUR RAGE? IT BLINDS YOU TO YOUR SURROUNDINGS.
RIGHT, SASUKE?
...
AND YOU'RE THE OFT-RUMORED BEAUTY SPY! WE SHOULD DO DINNER. ♡
OKUNI-SAN, WAS IT?
AND, OF COURSE...
... KYO-SAN.

YOU'RE LOOKING RATHER DOWN-TRODDEN.
HARDLY WORTH KILLING, I'D SAY ♡
SORRY TO KEEP YOU WAITING.

BUT HERE I AM!
酒

YOUR WORRIES ARE OVER ♡
Have a drink?

Kamijyo Circumstances

◉
Did you see the TV ad for "KYO"? Wow! Yup, there's a Kyo anime ad (*not a full anime, sorry)--it's being run as an ad for Magajin. Great to see Kyo in action! He's moving and grooving! And the best part is the COLOR.

It's really really cool, totally high-tech, really hip stuff!

It's running together with an anime clip of "GetBackers"--kind of "silent GB" versus "action Kyo." It looks great. If you haven't seen it, check it out!

he GB stuff's great, too!

*Note: The Kyo anime is now available in English on DVD!

Anonymous

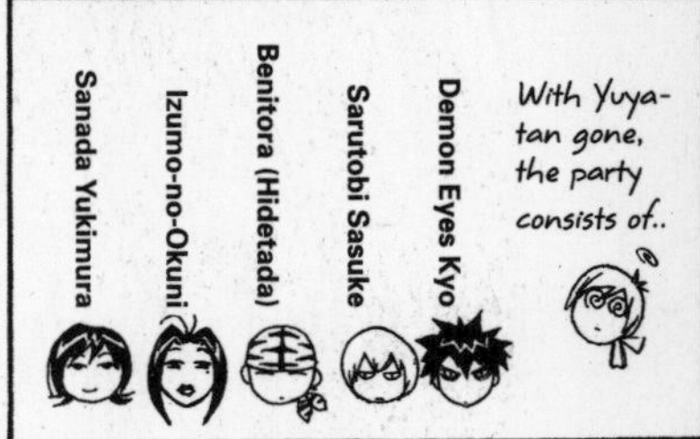

NO NEED TO WORRY, I'M HERE NOW. ♡
SAMURAI DEEPER KYO
CHAPTER FIFTY-NINE -- RUBBED THE WRONG WAY
YU... YUKIMURA-SAN!!!

HRM... I SEE.
SO YUYA-SAN HAS BEEN TAKEN HOS-TAGE.
WOULDN'T'VE EXPECTED THAT FROM THE TWELVE.
WELL, THEY CERTAINLY GOT YOU! ♡
WHAT'RE WE DOING SITTING HERE?!
WHAT IF SOMETHING HAPPENS TO YUYA-HAN?!
NO WORRIES. ♡
YUYA-HAN IS VERY IMPORTANT TO THE TWELVE. SHE'S THE ONLY THING KEEPING KYO AWAY.
ISN'T THAT RIGHT, KYO-SAN? ♡
HMM?
We'll talk later, Sasuke ♡
KYO-SAN UNDERSTANDS THAT. THAT'S WHY HE'S SO CALM.
....

HOW... HOW CA YOU BE SURE?!
I'M GOIN AHEAD... ALONE I I HAVE TO!
I CAN'T STAND THIS!!!
...
THE SLOPE OF HELL...
!
WHAZ-ZAT?
WHERE THEY WERE HEADED.
WHERE YUYA-SAN IS RIGHT NOW.

THE SLOPES ARE A PLACE WHERE DEATH AND LIFE WALK SIDE BY SIDE.

WE'VE WALKED FOR OVER AN HOUR, AND THE SCENERY'S THE SAME. I'VE LOST ALL SENSE OF DISTANCE AND TIME.

WHY ARE THEY SO ALERT?
...
サク
DEAR, OH DEAR ...
WE SEEM TO HAVE GONE IN A CIRCLE AGAIN.
HUH?
A CIRCLE ...?
はっ
WAIT!
THAT'S THE WREATH ANTERA GAVE ME!
THIS IS THE PLACE I WOKE UP!
BUT HOW? WE WALKED AN HOUR...
AAW, MAAAN!
STOP WHINING!
WELL...

さぁぁ…
I'M AFRAID WE'RE CAUGHT.
TRAPPED ON THE SLOPE.
TRAPPED?!
IT LOOKS LIKE GETTING TO THE LOTUS LAND WILL NOT BE SO EASY.
"THE SLOPE IS OF, AND NOT OF, THIS WORLD-- THOSE WHO ENTER WALK STRAIGHT TO HELL..."
PART OF A POEM KNOWN TO THOSE WHO LIVE IN THE FOREST. WHO KNOWS WHAT WAITS FOR US...
Y-YOU DON'T?
ガラ ガラ ガラ
AND THAT'S WHY I SAID...
ガラ ガラ ガラ
"THEY'RE GONNA GET STUCK AT THE SLOPE"...
BUT TORA-SAN JUST HAD TO GO!
ガラ ガラ ガラ
HA HAH ♥
Why I oughta...
YUYA-HAN'S IN EVEN MORE DANGER THEN!
And who said you could ride?!
NOW, NOW, NO NEED TO PANIC. I'M SURE SHE'S FINE!
YOU GOT TO LEARN TO RELAX, BONBON!
WHAT DO YOU CALL ME?!

WALK, PUNK!
AW, C'MON! HEY, YOU'RE SWERVING!
...
STRANGE... THEY'RE STILL FIGHTING, BUT NOT LIKE A MOMENT AGO.
I MAY BE SMALL, BUT EMOTIONALLY, I'M WAY OLDER THAN YOU.
I'M TOO PURE-HEARTED FOR YOU, THAT'S WHAT!
THAT TENSION... THAT RAGE. IT ALL SEEMS LIKE A DREAM.
I KNOW.
REALLY, YOU TWO!
I KNOW WHY THEY CHANGED.
SANADA YUKIMURA IS HERE.
UNFORTUNATELY, WOMEN DON'T LIKE PURE-HEARTED GUYS. ♡
Do they, Kyo?
WH-WHAT?!
WHO CARES WHAT THEY LIKE?
KYO-HAN? IS IT TRUE? SAY SOMETHING!
AH HAH! WHAT'S THE MATTER, KYO? CAT GOT YOUR TONGUE? SOMETHING!
YUKIMURA...
OKUNI-SAN! IS THAT YOU STARING AT ME? ♡
HAD ENOUGH OF KYO, HMM?
Looking for something new?
SILLY MAN.

LOOK, I PUT UP WITH A LOT OF LIP TILL NOW, BUT--
!!
ガラ
ガラ
ガラ
ガラ
ガラ
ガラ
ガラ
ガラ
ガラ
ガラ
ガラ
ガラ

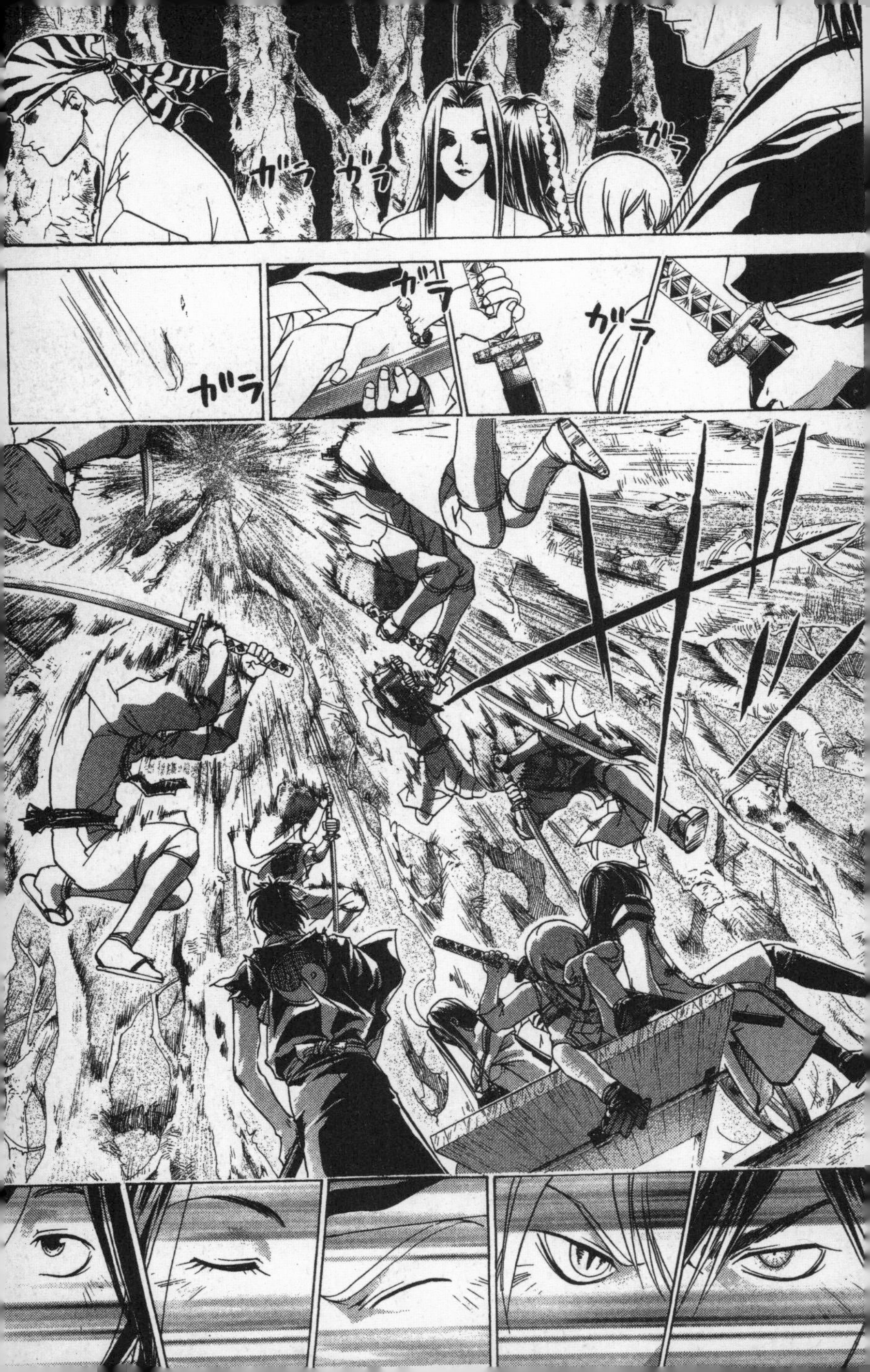
ガラ
ガラ ガラ
ガラ
ガラ
ガラ
ガラ

RAAAAAH!
WOW! ♡
YOU'VE A REALLY IMPROVE
YU-KIMUR SAN...
I'M FINE! ♡
I'M FINE! ♡
THEY CAN HANDLE THIS ONE. SAY...
...CARE FOR A DRINK? ♡
YUKI...
I DON'T BELIEVE THIS GUY!

HAAAH HAH HAH! BRILLIANT! YOU'VE FELLED MY MINIONS WITH EASE!
PEH!
DEMON EYES KYO, AND COMPANY, I PRESUME. I SEE WHY MEKIRA AND KUBIRA HAD IT ROUGH.
BUT WE ARE FAR STRONGER THAN THEM!
YOU FACE TWO OF THE TWELVE...
Skr-rrk
...HAIRA AND MAKORA!
...

TWO OF THE TWELV ?!
I HEARD YOU HAD A TUSSEL WITH SHINDARA'S CREW, YET YOU LOOK DOWNRIGHT... PEACHY!
ALL THE BETTER! IT WOULDN'T BE FUN TO PICK AT THEIR SCRAPS!
I PRESENT MY HOYOKU-HISHO! SLICE-AND-DICE TIME, GENTLEMEN!
GWAH HAH HAH HA!
WHA THE HE IS THA WEAP ON?
CAN YOU EVEN USE THOSE THINGS ?
UNH... UNH...
....

…
IT'S OKAY. YOU CAN RUN.
FEH!
A SOFTY, AS ALWAYS.
GO, QUICKLY.
WE WON'T GIVE CHASE.
UNH…
UGH…
UWAAAAH!
GAH!
AHHH!
AH AHH!

UWAAH!
FOOL!
NEVER TURN YOUR BACK TO YOUR ENEMY!
AND AFTER ALL THE TRAINING WASTED ON YOU.
YOU DIDN'T DESERVE TO LIVE.
HAH! SPINELESS COWARD!
YOU...

WHY DID YOU KILL HIM?!
HE WAS DONE FIGHTING, UNARMED!
HAH! ARE YOU A FOOL?!
THOSE WHO ARE OF NO USE DIE.
ALL MINIONS ARE THUS!
HE WAS A PAWN LIVING --AND YING-- FOR ME!
YUKIMURA ...
...
NEXT, IT'S YOUR TURN!
READY ...?!

...ARE YOU?
WHA -?
WHERE DID--?
I'M READY.

GWAAAAH!!!
GUH... UNH...
ONLY AN ARM? YOU MUST BE ONE OF THE TWELVE.
I meant to cut you in half.
LET ME TELL YOU SOMETHING...
...ABOUT ME.
I HATE PEOPLE WITH NO RESPECT FOR HUMAN LIFE...

AND THAT MEANS YOU.

To be continued...

STAFF

Yuzu Haruno (The Chief)
Hazuki Asami
Ken'ichi Suetake
Takaya Nagao
Akatsuki Soma
(in the order they came in)
Takiko Kamiya (Chapter Fifty-Eight)
Kumiko Sasaki (Chapter Fifty-Nine)

CHARACTER PROFILE

Profile please!

Sorry to keep y'all waiting ♡ I'm Sanada Saemonnosuke Yukimura, Age 37, Male, Height 170cm, Weight 53kg, B85-W70-H84, Foot Size: 26cm, Blood Type A, Occupation: Samurai, Birthplace: Kofu, in the Kai Domain.

Okay... No one really wanted to know your three sizes, there.

I've nothing to hide! ♡ I like women, sake, and...myself! How could anyone not like someone loved by Nobuyuki and the Sanada Ten? Dislikes...well, I guess I can do without boring people. Favorite foods... I eat anything, and as much of it as I want. I'm one of those people who can eat and not gain weight, see? ♡ Fears? Heh heh heh... Again, myself! And don't think I'm kidding around like Tora-san now.

So...you say you're 37? How come you look so young, then?

Well, I guess it's because I've got a mission. That, and I'm very skin-care-conscious ♡

Let's...not talk about skin. (Oh dear...)

Tee hee ♡. I'll leave it up to your imagination, then! ♡ To the fans, I'd like to say "enjoy adventuring with me!"

I give up.

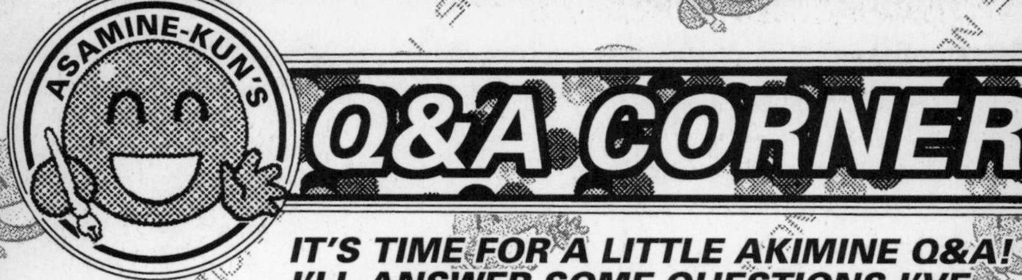

IT'S TIME FOR A LITTLE AKIMINE Q&A! I'LL ANSWER SOME QUESTIONS I'VE RECEIVED...

What about your profile, Kamijyo-sensei?

Akimine Kamijyo: born 9/13. Virgo. My hobby was drawing manga. I don't have other hobbies. That is, I don't have time ;-).

What do you listen to while you work?

I let the top 10 radio play...or listen to CDs and MDs the staff members bring in. I don't have any particular favorites, but I do kind of like The Yellow Monkey and Shiina Ringo--sort of J-Rock stuff. And I like good lyrics.

I'm no good at Japanese History. How about you, Kamijyo-sensei?

Sorry, I elected World History in high school ;-). However, I'm studying a lot right now. I recently realized that, more than memorizing time charts and events, it's more interesting to learn what kind of people lived way back when and what sorts of things those people did together. The phrase "historical figure" means a lot more to me now. This has helped me enjoy Japanese history much more.

I HOPE I ANSWERED YOUR QUESTIONS. SEND MORE! THANKS

CHALLENGE AKIMINE KAMIJYO

Tiffany B.
Concord, NC
Age 15

You're right—Yukiumua sure is hot! But are you sure that's him and not his double?

Daniella G.
Miami, FL
Age 12

Is that a spider in your cleavage, or do you just want to kill me? Seriously, great Mahiro pic. I hope she'll be back soon!

Celebrity Fan Art!

From the artist for The Kindaichi Casefiles... It's a postcard from Fumiya Sato-sensei!

***Sorry, Kamijyo-sensei!* --Fumiya Sato**

***The Heart of a Maiden**

Jayme S.

You are a sick, sick person... but I love it! Although in a way, it makes sense... Kyo's clearly in love with himself, and if he is starting to think of Kyoshiro's body as his own... Long live shonen-ai!

Leigh H.

Absolutely stunning! This must be the most detailed fan art I've ever received. Thank you so much!

Jeanenne C.

I never could figure out how to tie those damn things. I really like the demon behind Kyo's head. Very dramatic.

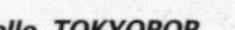

This
month
receiv
a mo
unusu
reque
from f
of ou
reade
Exam
their
close
and ju
for
yours

Jeremy G.

Ah, the deadly White Crow. Nice use of chiaroscuro shading techniques for a realistic look but I said CONSUMMATE Vs! Consummate! Ai yai yai...

Hello, TOKYOPOP,

We five of Manga and Anime Club are sending you our Samurai Deeper Kyo fan art in hopes you can help us. Sure we would all love to see each of our projects published, but the reason we sent five different pieces is this: we are in need of guidance. We have many braves and no chief. Could you tell us which of the submissions represents the best work of the five (this way we know who will lead us as president of the club). Simply, you tell us which of the projects is the best and we then elect the person who was head of the development of that project as our leader. J

With warmest regards,
Manga and Anime Club
Shattuck-St. Mary's School
Faribault, MN

David W.

At last, a manly man's Kyo! If Kyo were making the deciding vote, I'm sure he'd go with this one.

ichael L.
embroke Pines, FL

hat is this, Florida month? ice to see Kyo has so many ns in the panhandle.

Mariann M.
Pinon Hills, CA
Age 16

A kindler, gentler Benitora. Cuteness with a spear. I like it!

Kyle L.
Stuart, FL

Notice how the blood clings to the demonically charged Muramasa blade!

THANK YOU FOR ALL THE AMAZING ART! PLEASE KEEP SENDING IT!

Message from the Editor:

♡

New guidelines! Please read carefully

How to submit:

1) Send your work via regular mail (NOT e-mail) to:

SAMURAI DEEPER KYO FAN MAIL
C/O TOKYOPOP
5900 WILSHIRE BLVD., SUITE 2000
LOS ANGELES, CA 90036

2) All work should be in black-and-white and no larger than 8.5" x 11". (And try not to fold it too many times!) 3) Anything you send will not be returned. If you want to keep your original, it's fine to send us a copy. 4) Please include your full name, age, city and state for us to print with your work. If you'd rather us use a pen name, please include that too. 5) IMPORTANT: If you're under the age of 18, you must have your parent's permission in order for us to print your work. Any submissions without a signed note of parental consent will not be used. 6) For full details, please check out *http://www.tokyopop.com/aboutus/fanart.php*

Disclaimer: Anything you send to us becomes the property of TOKYOPOP Inc. and will not be returned to you. We will have the right to print, reproduce, distribute or modify the artwork for use in future volumes of Samurai Deeper Kyo or on the Web without payment to you.

GLOSSARY

Aokigahara—The forest at the base of Mt. Fuji. It's reputation for being haunted lives on to this day.

Edo Era—(1603-1868) Japan's "golden era" of political and economic stability after the civil wars of the Sengoku Era. During the Edo Era, all Japan would be ruled by one Shogun. Samurai Deeper Kyo takes place at the start of the Edo Era.

-han—the "-san" suffix as said with Benitora's kansai-ben inflection.

Kansai-ben—Regional dialect of the Kansai era (Osaka, Kyoto, Kobe). Benitora speaks with this dialect, known for its fast-paced diction and unique slang.

-kun—An honorific label used when addressing close friends or children. Usually used toward boys.

Muramasa—Muramasa was the name of the student to the great sword maker Masamune in Japanese history, turned myth. Muramasa was known as the insane and violent match of his gentle and peaceful master. It is said the swords he forged would bring out the bloodlust from their wielders.

Oneechan/Ne-chan (pronounced nay-chan)—Literally, "older sister." Also used by children toward a young woman. Sasuke uses the familiar "-chan," to be friendly, and at the same time to belittle Yuya.

-sama—Honorific denoting the person is of a much higher status than the speaker. Similar to "lord" or "master" in English.

-san—The most common honorific. Similar to "Mr./Mrs."

Sanada Clan—During Sekigahara, Sanada Masayuki (Yukimura's father), fought against the Tokugawa. Sanada Nobuyuki (Yukimura's brother—see SDK vol. 4) sided with Tokugawa, and after the war was able to use his influence to save his father and brother's lives. Sanada Yukimura continued to fight against the Tokugawa after Sekigahara. He and his ten warriors, the Sanada Ju-Yushi, have since passed into legend.

Sarutobi Sasuke—One of the Sanada Ten and a legendary ninja.

Sekigahara—The greatest battle in Japanese history, the Battle of Sekigahara took place in the fall of 1600 and ended years of civil war.

Shogun—The supreme ruler of a united Japan during the Edo Era.

-tan—the "-chan" suffix as said with Benitora's kansai-ben inflection.

Tokugawa Hidetada —The historical first shogun of Japan.

Tokugawa Ieyasu —The son of the Shogun and second shogun of Japan, here fictionalized as Benitora.

utsusemi—The ninja-technique of substitution. It involves replacing one's own body with a fake (usually a chunk of wood), which distracts your attacker long enough to get a good hit in.

A nightmare on the Slope of Hell... The killer of Yuya's brother revealed at last!

Anything can happen, and it does in SDK, Volume 8! Don't miss it!!!

TOKYOPOP

Welcome to the school dance...

Try the punch.

BATTLE VIXENS

OT
OLDER TEEN
AGE 16+

© 2004 Yuji Shiozaki. ©2004 TOKYOPOP Inc. All rights reserved.

www.TOKYOPOP.com

ALSO AVAILABLE FROM TOKYOPOP®

TA-TEN
LANET LADDER
LANETES
RIEST
RINCESS AI
SYCHIC ACADEMY
UEEN'S KNIGHT, THE
AGNAROK
AVE MASTER
EALITY CHECK
EBIRTH
EBOUND
EMOTE
SING STARS OF MANGA
ABER MARIONETTE J
AILOR MOON
AINT TAIL
AIYUKI
AMURAI DEEPER KYO
AMURAI GIRL REAL BOUT HIGH SCHOOL
CRYED
EIKAI TRILOGY, THE
GT. FROG
HAOLIN SISTERS
HIRAHIME-SYO: SNOW GODDESS TALES
HUTTERBOX
KULL MAN, THE
NOW DROP
ORCERER HUNTERS
TONE
UIKODEN III
UKI
HREADS OF TIME
OKYO BABYLON
OKYO MEW MEW
OKYO TRIBES
RAMPS LIKE US
NDER THE GLASS MOON
AMPIRE GAME
SION OF ESCAFLOWNE, THE
ARRIORS OF TAO
ILD ACT
ISH
ORLD OF HARTZ
DAY
ODIAC P.I.

OVELS

LAMP SCHOOL PARANORMAL INVESTIGATORS
ARMA CLUB
AILOR MOON
LAYERS

RT BOOKS

RT OF CARDCAPTOR SAKURA
RT OF MAGIC KNIGHT RAYEARTH, THE
EACH: MIWA UEDA ILLUSTRATIONS

ANIME GUIDES

COWBOY BEBOP
GUNDAM TECHNICAL MANUALS
SAILOR MOON SCOUT GUIDES

TOKYOPOP KIDS

STRAY SHEEP

CINE-MANGA™

ALADDIN
CARDCAPTORS
DUEL MASTERS
FAIRLY ODDPARENTS, THE
FAMILY GUY
FINDING NEMO
G.I. JOE SPY TROOPS
GREATEST STARS OF THE NBA
JACKIE CHAN ADVENTURES
JIMMY NEUTRON: BOY GENIUS, THE ADVENTURES OF
KIM POSSIBLE
LILO & STITCH: THE SERIES
LIZZIE MCGUIRE
LIZZIE MCGUIRE MOVIE, THE
MALCOLM IN THE MIDDLE
POWER RANGERS: DINO THUNDER
POWER RANGERS: NINJA STORM
PRINCESS DIARIES 2
RAVE MASTER
SHREK 2
SIMPLE LIFE, THE
SPONGEBOB SQUAREPANTS
SPY KIDS 2
SPY KIDS 3-D: GAME OVER
THAT'S SO RAVEN
TOTALLY SPIES
TRANSFORMERS: ARMADA
TRANSFORMERS: ENERGON
VAN HELSING

For more information visit www.TOKYOPOP.com

03.30.04T

ALSO AVAILABLE FROM 

MANGA

.HACK//LEGEND OF THE TWILIGHT
@LARGE
ABENOBASHI: MAGICAL SHOPPING ARCADE
A.I. LOVE YOU
AI YORI AOSHI
ANGELIC LAYER
ARM OF KANNON
BABY BIRTH
BATTLE ROYALE
BATTLE VIXENS
BRAIN POWERED
BRIGADOON
B'TX
CANDIDATE FOR GODDESS, THE
CARDCAPTOR SAKURA
CARDCAPTOR SAKURA - MASTER OF THE CLOW
CHOBITS
CHRONICLES OF THE CURSED SWORD
CLAMP SCHOOL DETECTIVES
CLOVER
COMIC PARTY
CONFIDENTIAL CONFESSIONS
CORRECTOR YUI
COWBOY BEBOP
COWBOY BEBOP: SHOOTING STAR
CRAZY LOVE STORY
CRESCENT MOON
CROSS
CULDCEPT
CYBORG 009
D•N•ANGEL
DEMON DIARY
DEMON ORORON, THE
DEUS VITAE
DIABOLO
DIGIMON
DIGIMON TAMERS
DIGIMON ZERO TWO
DOLL
DRAGON HUNTER
DRAGON KNIGHTS
DRAGON VOICE
DREAM SAGA
DUKLYON: CLAMP SCHOOL DEFENDERS
EERIE QUEERIE!
ERICA SAKURAZAWA: COLLECTED WORKS
ET CETERA
ETERNITY
EVIL'S RETURN
FAERIES' LANDING
FAKE
FLCL
FLOWER OF THE DEEP SLEEP
FORBIDDEN DANCE
FRUITS BASKET
G GUNDAM
GATEKEEPERS
GETBACKERS
GIRL GOT GAME
GIRLS' EDUCATIONAL CHARTER
GRAVITATION
GTO
GUNDAM BLUE DESTINY
GUNDAM SEED ASTRAY
GUNDAM WING
GUNDAM WING: BATTLEFIELD OF PACIFISTS
GUNDAM WING: ENDLESS WALTZ
GUNDAM WING: THE LAST OUTPOST (G-UNIT)
GUYS' GUIDE TO GIRLS
HANDS OFF!
HAPPY MANIA
HARLEM BEAT
HONEY MUSTARD
I.N.V.U.
IMMORTAL RAIN
INITIAL D
INSTANT TEEN: JUST ADD NUTS
ISLAND
JING: KING OF BANDITS
JING: KING OF BANDITS - TWILIGHT TALES
JULINE
KARE KANO
KILL ME, KISS ME
KINDAICHI CASE FILES, THE
KING OF HELL
KODOCHA: SANA'S STAGE
LAMENT OF THE LAMB
LEGAL DRUG
LEGEND OF CHUN HYANG, THE
LES BIJOUX
LOVE HINA
LUPIN III
LUPIN III: WORLD'S MOST WANTED
MAGIC KNIGHT RAYEARTH I
MAGIC KNIGHT RAYEARTH II
MAHOROMATIC: AUTOMATIC MAIDEN
MAN OF MANY FACES
MARMALADE BOY
MARS
MARS: HORSE WITH NO NAME
MINK
MIRACLE GIRLS
MIYUKI-CHAN IN WONDERLAND
MODEL
MY LOVE
NECK AND NECK
ONE
ONE I LOVE, THE
PARADISE KISS
PARASYTE
PASSION FRUIT
PEACH GIRL
PEACH GIRL: CHANGE OF HEART
PET SHOP OF HORRORS

03.30.04T

CANBY PUBLIC LIBRARY
292 N. HOLLY
CANBY, OR 97013

STOP!

This is the back of the book. You wouldn't want to spoil a great ending!

This book is printed "manga-style," in the authentic Japanese right-to-left format. Since none of the artwork has been flipped or altered, readers get to experience the story just as the creator intended. You've been asking for it, so TOKYOPOP® delivered: authentic, hot-off-the-press, and far more fun!

DIRECTIONS

If this is your first time reading manga-style, here's a quick guide to help you understand how it works.

It's easy... just start in the top right panel and follow the numbers. Have fun, and look for more 100% authentic manga from TOKYOPOP®!